Wildlife Images of the

ADIRONDACKS

Wildlife Images of the
ADIRONDACKS

Eric Dresser

North Country Books, Inc.
Utica, New York

above *Common loon on Forked Lake*
previous page *Doe and newborn fawn near McKeever*

To Kathy, the love of my life.
Thank you for all your love, patience,
confidence, and encouragement. Thank you
for being my soul mate and for allowing
me to pursue my dream career.

Preface

As a young boy, while fishing with my father, a seed of appreciation for the outdoors was planted. Today that appreciation has become a lifelong passion. A fishing trip with my dad was more than fishing. He would always find the time to stop and point out wildflowers, birds, insects, and anything else that caught his observant eye. He taught me to do more than just look; he taught me to see.

Fishing trips in the Adirondacks were always my favorites. It wasn't because the fishing was better there, it was because of the places we went. Places like Raquette River, Saranac River, Black River, and Taylor Pond to name a few. Places where you could find true wilderness. Places where you may not hear a vehicle for the entire day. Places where the landscape was rugged and spellbinding.

Such vivid memories of the Adirondacks continued to draw me back to the area as I grew older. On one particularly memorable trip, my nephew Jeff and I were camping on Moss Lake. As the orange glow of another breathtaking Adirondack sunset faded, I told Jeff "we had better get to sleep because we have to pack up our gear early tomorrow morning and head back to everyday life."

The next morning we were awakened by the sound of thunder echoing off the hills in the pre-dawn light. We scrambled to life so we could get everything packed up while it was still dry. We got the last of our gear into our backpacks just as a few sprinkles started. Then it happened.

As the thunder got closer and louder, two loons started their mournful yodeling. I was listening to the echoing thunder and loons, thinking to myself that it doesn't get any better then this, when a group of coyotes chimed in. It was a magical serenade!

That was about twenty years ago and the sound is as lucid in my mind as if I were still standing there. Experiences such as these are what inspire me to return time and time again to photograph Adirondack wildlife. Such is the mystical draw of the Adirondacks.

–Eric Dresser

above *Eastern bluebird, Tupper Lake*
opposite *The muskrat on the bottom had no reaction as the other climbed over the top and continued on its way*
previous page *I came across this black bear while hiking near Cascade Lake in the Pigeon Lake Wilderness Area*

above *Skipper butterfly photographed early in the morning while it was still chilled from the nighttime cold*
opposite *Gray tree frogs are amazing climbers; I spotted this one while hiking in the Pigeon Lake Wilderness Area*

above While harmless, milk snakes can be quite aggressive and rather intimidating
opposite Fawns have lost their spots by autumn and no longer depend on their mother for milk

Snow bunting near the town of Saranac, Clinton County
A beaver enjoying a snack on an unusually warm late-winter day

above *The mink is nearly as quick and agile in water as it is on land*
opposite *Young bull moose, Moose River Plains*

above *River otters investigate my blind from a spring hole in the ice*
opposite *The nomadic snowy owl can sometimes be found in the Adirondacks during the winter months, although it breeds and spends its summer much farther north*

above *If you've ever sat around an Adirondack campfire at night, you may have seen a deer mouse scurrying about*
opposite *This wood duck hen seems to be quite infatuated with this fortunate drake*

23

above *While the majority of moths fly at night, the hummingbird moth is active during the day*
opposite *Great-crested flycatcher, Moss Lake*

above *Canada goose goslings at the Tupper Lake boat launch*
opposite *An alert doe and fawn*

29

above *With eyes as sharp as its beak, the great blue heron is a formidable hunter*
opposite *A friend in Old Forge told me about this raccoon that was feeding on birdseed that fell from his feeder*

above *This image was taken in mid-August when a friend noticed these snowshoe hare bunnies in his garden*
opposite *This inquisitive red fox pup was very photogenic*

above Common loon nest on Horseshoe Lake
opposite Young black bear, Essex County

above *Moose, like this cow and calf, are making a slow but steady comeback in the Adirondacks*
opposite *This male wild turkey is attempting to seduce a mate by fanning his tail and puffing up his feathers*

above *Snow geese leaving a field in the Champlain Valley*
opposite *After a long winter, the sound of honking geese returning north is welcome*

above With the whitetail's breeding season winding down, this buck shed one antler a week after this photo was taken
opposite Bold and brazen, the red squirrel is the most plentiful squirrel in wilderness areas of the Adirondacks

above *With coloration that mimics that of a monarch, the viceroy is often wrongly identified at first glance, but a closer look reveals the distinguishing curved black line crossing the veins of the hind wing*
opposite *The red eft is a newt, which, unlike a salamander, has dry and rough skin*

above Great egrets on the North Branch of Moose River in Old Forge
opposite The barred owl inhabits the Adirondacks throughout the year

above *The male ruffed grouse beats his wings creating a sound intended to make other grouse aware of his presence*
opposite *I called this Lewis County bull moose by making the sound of a cow moose*

above *Scarlet tanager near Moss Lake*
opposite *White-tailed doe and flowers, Champlain Valley*
previous pages *The ponds created by beavers provide excellent habitat for many forms of wildlife*

above *I noticed this snail while hiking a trail to Windfall Pond in Herkimer County*
opposite *Snapping turtle on the edge of Rondaxe Road*

above This cottontail rabbit was soaking up the warmth of the sun near Port Henry
opposite Bald eagle over Big Moose Lake

The American woodcock is found in forests where it uses its long bill to probe the mud for worms
Contrary to its name, the fisher does not hunt for fish; they are nearly as agile in a tree as on the ground

above *Short-tailed shrew investigates a shed deer antler*
opposite *Porcupines can't throw their quills, instead they have to be directly contacted*

58

above *Hooded merganser hen*
opposite *This 11-point buck had recently shed the velvet covering from his antlers*

above *Pileated woodpecker chicks in the Five Ponds Wilderness Area*
opposite *This cedar waxwing nest was in the backyard of a friend's camp in Herkimer County*

63

above This chipmunk was busily gathering nesting material and a store of food for the approaching winter
opposite North America's only marsupial, the opossum

above Pied-billed grebe with chicks near the inlet of Big Moose Lake
opposite Striped skunk near Nelson Lake, Herkimer County

above *The ring-necked snake is a small woodland snake, typically found by rolling over stones or logs*
opposite *Red fox lured into camera range with the use of a predator call*

above *This red-breasted nuthatch was photographed near a friend's bird feeder in Old Forge*
opposite *Mallard drake over the Moose River, near Rondaxe Road*

above Whitetail fawns often bed alone; their spots act as camouflage and they have far less scent than their mother
opposite Red-shouldered hawks often hunt from dead branches where they have an unobstructed view of the forest floor
previous pages River otters heading for a spring hole in the ice

above *By moving my kayak ever so slowly, I was able to close the distance and watch as this green heron hunted from a fallen tree in the Raquette River*
opposite *Woodchuck near West Canada Creek, Herkimer County*

above *American toad, Tupper Lake*
opposite *American woodcock with her well-camouflaged chicks*

above Female northern harrier hunting over a beaver meadow in Herkimer County
opposite This moose was photographed in a Lewis County pasture; the lovesick bull was fascinated with the heifers

above *Crab spider near Moss Lake parking area*
opposite *The common loon is a true icon of the Adirondacks; its plaintive calls can be heard on many lakes from early spring through autumn*

above *Pine grosbeak eating crab apples, Champlain Valley*
opposite *The gray squirrel prefers areas with a good number of nut-bearing trees—or bird feeders*

above Green-winged teal on a beaver pond in Herkimer County
opposite I photographed this springtime beaver north of Nelson Lake near McKeever

above Red fox near the entrance of its den
opposite Bald eagle perched along the Hudson River, near the hamlet of North Creek

above *Blackburnian warblers are quite common in Adirondack forests throughout the summer*
opposite *The Acadian hairstreak is such a quick and erratic flier that one has a difficult time keeping track of its whereabouts*

above *American widgeon, Utowana Lake in Hamilton County*
opposite *This is a captive Lynx; biologists reintroduced eighty eight Lynx into the Adirondacks from 1989 to 1991, but sadly, it is believed none survived*

95

above American bittern male in courtship display near Cedar River Flow
opposite The greater distance between the ears indicates this black bear is older than the one pictured on page 34
previous pages Painted turtles sunbathing on a beaver pond near Tupper Lake

above Mink on the bank of Bear Creek
opposite This large buck is marking his territory in the Pigeon Lake Wilderness Area, Herkimer County

above Noticing this blue dasher dragonfly had a preferred resting spot, I waited for him to venture out over South Pond and I quickly took up position; after a brief wait, he returned to his favorite perch and this photo was taken opposite A red fox pup perfects its hunting skills by pouncing on nearly anything near its den

above A rough-legged hawk flies low over a beaver meadow after a vole has eluded its talons
opposite Hooded merganser drakes on the Little Ausable

105

above *Bounding doe near West Canada Creek*
opposite *Eastern coyote on its evening hunt, Champlain Valley*

above To photograph this wood duck, I covered myself and my gear with camouflage cloth and sat concealed on the bank of a narrow beaver pond near McKeever
opposite This raccoon, near Inlet, was taking advantage of a warm afternoon—a welcome break from winter's severity

above Horned lark atop a roadside snow bank near West Canada Creek
opposite Also called a varying hare, the snowshoe hare changes from brown in the summer to white in the winter

above *Spotted salamander*
opposite *I came upon this black-throated green warbler near the Oswegatchie River*

above *Two bucks sparring to establish pecking order and breeding rights*
opposite *Far less common than the ruffed grouse, the spruce grouse is also found in the Adirondacks*

above The polyphemus moth has an impressive wingspan of up to six inches
opposite Rough-legged hawk with a vole

above *Mallard drake over the Moose River, near Rondaxe Road*
opposite *I lured this gray fox into camera range using a call that imitates a rabbit in distress*

above *Turkey Vulture sunning itself along Route 30 north of Blue Mountain*

opposite *I captured this image of a black bear from my vehicle in the Inlet area*

previous pages *By moving this garter snake to a new location I was able to capture this image showing its tongue*

above This beaver may have depleted his winter supply of food;
I spotted him dragging this sapling north of Tupper Lake in mid-March
opposite Great gray owls are only seen in the Adirondacks when their winter food supply runs low farther north

above *Wild turkey gobbling near McKeever*
opposite *Cow moose at first light alongside Rondaxe Road*

above Common merganser drake, St. Regis canoe wilderness
opposite Canada geese mate for life; the nest site is chosen by the female and she accepts all incubation duties

above *Semipalmated plover photographed from my kayak, Stillwater Reservoir*
opposite *Great horned owl*

above *The winter wren is found in wet shaded woods—often near beaver ponds*
opposite *This chipmunk is busily gathering food after a long winter*

Male osprey building a nest
Loud in color and in voice, this blue jay was photographed near a bird feeder

above The coloration of this "piebald" button buck is caused by a recessive genetic trait
opposite Young bull moose, Moose River Plains

Observing Adirondack Wildlife

Say the name Adirondack Park, and most will think of the breathtaking beauty of the mountains, endless forests, streams, lakes, and ponds. However, the park is also home to many wild creatures.

Included in this book are images of these wild residents of the park. Some are seen throughout the year while others are seen only at certain times. Below are some general tips for those with an interest in observing or photographing these creatures.

I frequently refer to field guides, which can be helpful in locating an animal's preferred habitat as well as in identifying a creature once you see it.

Medium to high quality binoculars will allow close observation from a greater distance. Binoculars are available in many sizes, shapes, and powers. All are designated with two numbers such as 7 x 35 or 10 x 50. The first number represents the power or magnification of the binocular and the second number is the size of the objective lens. Larger objective lenses gather more light and normally produce far less eye strain for the user. My favorite binoculars are 8 x 42 roof-prism design. They are relatively light to carry and easy to hold steady.

Once in the field we must learn to slow our pace.

To this day I must remind myself to slow down. By walking slowly and stopping often you will find many inconspicuous subjects that would have certainly been overlooked had we hurried through an area. It is easier to distinguish the subtle movements of creatures in the field when we remain stationary. On the other hand, if we are constantly moving, wildlife will be much more likely to detect our presence and vanish before we catch a glimpse. Their existence demands that. It must be remembered that we are now in the home of nature's creatures and they will detect things which look out of place as easily as we do in our own homes.

Learn to look for things that appear out of the ordinary. For instance, tall grass or brush moving on a calm morning may be caused by a grouse traveling through the area. "Seeing" is a matter of being observant and picking out subtle details. It takes more than good eyesight and can only be developed through concentration and experience.

Direction of travel and route taken are very important. As I move through an area I like to look ahead and plan a route that offers some sort of cover. Anything that will break my silhouette, such as thick brush or trees, will be chosen as a place to stop and observe. Many mammals, such as deer, bears, and fox, have a very acute sense of smell. For this reason it is advisable to walk into the wind whenever possible. We may occasionally get lucky and fool a deer's eyes or ears, but the nose knows.

Unlike mammals, most birds have a poor sense of smell. Compensation for their shortcoming in smell is their extremely keen eyesight. We can better our chances of remaining unseen by wearing natural or drab colored clothing.

Spending as much time as possible out-of-doors

Great blue heron on Raquette Lake

is the best tip that can be offered to those wishing to take a closer look at wildlife. Whether observing or photographing wildlife, luck is the product of persistence. Through experiences gained you will develop favorite strategies of your own. You will also become more familiar with certain areas and will soon learn the travel patterns and favored locations of local wildlife. Move slowly and be observant, taking notice of tracks, droppings, food sources, dens, and wildlife sightings. These will, when combined, offer the clues needed to choose a productive area for future ventures.

Acknowledgements

First, I must thank my father, who introduced me to the Adirondacks as a young boy. He sparked and fueled my passion for the natural world. Words can't describe just how much I miss him. Thanks to Mom and my sister Diane for your encouragement, understanding, and love.

I am indebted to Rob Igoe, Jr., and Zach Steffen of North Country Books. Without their help, this book would have never come to fruition. Thanks to all my friends and acquaintances who have conveyed their confidence in my photography.

And finally, thanks to my photographer buddies Nick Kalathas, Todd Harmon, and Chris Kayler for their enthusiasm, inspiration, laughs, and memories shared in the field.

Photography and text © Eric Dresser 2011

Editing: Zach Steffen and Rob Igoe, Jr.
Design: Zach Steffen and Rob Igoe, Jr.
Prepress File Preparation: Nancy Did It!

ISBN-10 1-59531-026-6
ISBN-13 978-1-59531-026-2

Printed in China

Library of Congress Cataloging-in-Publication Data

Dresser, Eric.
  Wildlife images of the Adirondacks / Eric Dresser.
    p. cm.
  ISBN-13: 978-1-59531-026-2 (alk. paper)
  ISBN-10: 1-59531-026-6 (alk. paper)
  1. Wildlife photography--New York (State)--Adirondack Mountains.
2. Animals--New York (State)--Adirondack Mountains--Pictorial works. I. Title.
  TR727.D723 2010
  779'.32097475--dc22

            2010002414

Visit Eric Dresser's Web site: http://ecdphoto.addr.com/

Published by North Country Books, Inc.
220 Lafayette Street • Utica, NY 13502
(315) 735-4877 • Orders: (800) 342-7409
www.northcountrybooks.com